Cantonese Cuisine:

A Bite of Freshness & Naturalness

Elegant Guangdong Series Editorial Board

CONTENTS

Food Traditions
Folk Customs

Local Specialties
Fruit and Tea

Foreword

Guangdong Province, located in the south of China's Nanling Mountain Range on the South China Sea coast, borders Hong Kong and Macao Special Administrative Regions to the south. It also leads the country in terms of Gross Domestic Product (GDP) and population. The fascinating region, which has a long rich history, vast land areas and a long coastal line, is set to embrace a brand–new future. Guangdong people have always been the bellwether and forerunner in various fields, whether in expanding maritime trade, or moving on to modern civilization, or promoting reform and opening up.

Guangdong food remained obscure for a long time in ancient China. The economy of Lingnan Region (south of the Five Ridges) has seen robust development since the Tang and Song Dynasties (618–1279) as China's economic center moved southward and the advanced technologies in the Central Plains reached the southern part of the country. Lingnan became the wealthiest region in China during the Qing Dynasty (1644–1911) due to the Canton Trade System (1757–1842) which made Guangzhou become China's only port for Western trade. It's a principle that business prosperity always leads to booming of catering. Guangzhou emerged as one of the world's largest trading ports and a vibrant international metropolis during the Qing Dynasty. Consequently, the city became a capital of gastronomy.

Stir-fried rice noodles with beef

Cantonese morning tea dimsum

People regard food as their primary want, and it's a natural right to be a foodie. Sun Yat-sen, the forerunner of China's revolution to end feudalism, once said, "Delicious food should also be viewed as artworks since good-looking things and pleasant musical notes are both artworks." Guangdong people have created so many wonders to satisfy foodies' passion for delicacies. Gourmet food embodies the most robust part of Guangdong's culture. Fine traits in Guangdong people's disposition, such as pioneering spirit, open-mindedness, inclusiveness and pragmatism, are all reflected in their food culture.

Guangdong, located in the subtropical zone, has a mild climate and abundant rainfall year round. As a result, there are always bounties of fresh vegetables and fruits in all seasons, laying a solid foundation for its being a paradise for gourmet food. Cantonese cuisine is composed of Guangfu, Teochew and Hakka cuisines, due to the distinct culinary customs of the three branches of the Han ethnic group—Guangfu people, Chaoshan people and Hakka people. These categories of Cantonese cuisine demonstrate three different styles of life: Guangfu people, who reside in the most fertile Pearl River Delta Region and enjoy abundant food materials for cooking; Chaoshan people (in great Chaozhou–Shantou area), who live in the coastal areas of eastern Guangdong, focus on seafood dishes; Hakka people, most of whom live in mountainous areas, highlight raw materials from mountains in cooking.

Shunde sashimi

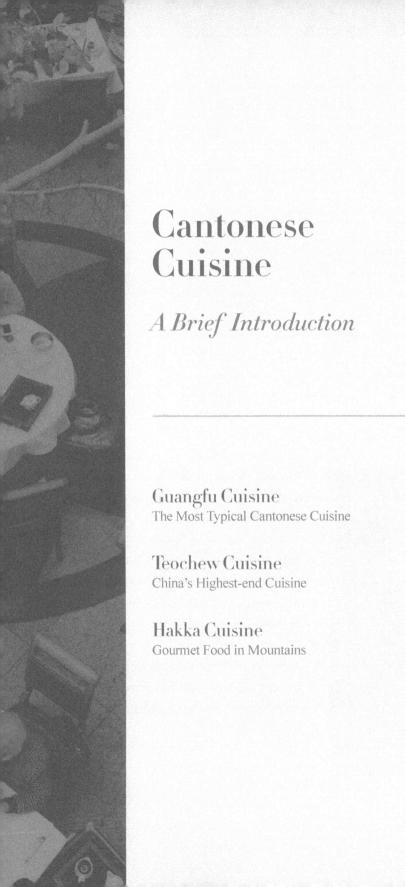

Cantonese Cuisine

A Brief Introduction

Guangfu Cuisine
The Most Typical Cantonese Cuisine

Teochew Cuisine
China's Highest-end Cuisine

Hakka Cuisine
Gourmet Food in Mountains

Guangfu Cuisine
The Most Typical Cantonese Cuisine

The three categories of Cantonese cuisine (also called "Yue cuisine" nowadays) feature different characteristics.

Guangfu cuisine was renamed Guangzhou cuisine in the 1960s and 1970s. Originating in Guangzhou, it is the most typical Cantonese cuisine.

Guangfu cuisine is like transformers in animated films that can change themselves into different objects in a dazzling way.

BeiYuan Restaurant faithfully depicts the details of a Lingnan-style Chinese garden

Braised sea shrimp in Cantonese style

Guangfu cuisine incorporates Nanhai, Panyu, Dongguan, Shunde and Zhongshan cuisines, featuring a combination of relatively light, fresh, clear and fragrant flavors. In this culinary style, dishes are cooked in different ways in different seasons, with light flavors served in summer and autumn and mellow flavors in winter and spring.

Using an extensive variety of ingredients and retaining fresh taste are the two greatest features of Guangfu cuisine. Other distinctive features are as follows: proportions of ingredients are meticulous, condiments are varied and ingenious, and decorations of food are beautiful and brightly colored. The culinary style subtly blends the essence of cuisines in different cities and regions, including Beijing, Suzhou, Yangzhou and Hangzhou, as well as the western cooking techniques. Chefs are good at innovation based on imitation, integrating different culinary styles to form their special features and thus bringing about more varieties of dishes. Early in 1965, a total of 5,457 kinds of dishes in Guangfu cuisine were showcased at the Guangzhou Famous Dishes and Delicious Desserts Expo. Guangfu cuisine also features upscale dishes, such as the exquisite banquet of edible bird's nest and shark's fin, but there are more family-style dishes, such as white gourd soup and long-simmered soup.

The cooking techniques include stir-frying, frying, sautéing, braising, soft-frying, stewing, boiling, steaming, pickling, spicing and curing with salt or sugar. The most typical dishes include white boiled shrimp, roast suckling pig, braised sliced pork with taro, Huangpu scrambled egg and stewed tylorrhynchus.

Cantonese crispy duck

Teochew Cuisine
China's Highest-end Cuisine

Teochew cuisine, a counterpart of Guangfu cuisine, is usually regarded as the top cuisine in China. It is dubbed "China's highest-end cuisine."

The great Chaozhou–Shantou area, located in the subtropical zone, faces the sea to its south with abundant marine products. As the Chinese saying goes that "Those living near the sea live off the sea", Teochew cuisine is well-known for its seafood cooking techniques. Selection of ingredients is meticulous and curing procedures are elaborate. Seafood dishes, served with various fragrant sauces, are fresh and delicious, refreshing but not light, fragrant without fishy smell, and mellow but not greasy. Some of the signature dishes include crab paste like mandarin duck, lobster with lettuce, stewed shark's fin, oyster omelette, boiled eels and consommé crab balls.

Raw pickled crab

Teochew cuisine focuses on both meat and vegetable dishes. Chefs are adept at cooking dishes with vegetables and fruits. Raw materials are cooked with delicate skills to create fresh, refreshing, delicious and nutritious dishes. Teochew dishes commended by foodies include the "Protect Country Dish" favored by Zhao Bing, the last emperor of the Southern Song Dynasty (1127–1279), smashed water chestnut, braised mushroom and leaf mustard and sweet potato stewed with sugar.

Shantou seafood stall

Teochew cuisine is a kaleidoscope of dishes and flavors. Apart from seafood and assorted spiced meat, there are more than 100 varieties of cold dishes, such as pickles, kale borecole and dried radish, as well as over 100 kinds of meat balls, with the most famous ones being beef meat balls and fish balls. Teochew-style hot pot and light soup are also well-known.

Teochew cuisine enjoys a high reputation, partly because the cutting techniques are exquisite and curing procedures are elaborate. The processing methods vary according to the traits of raw materials. Cooking skills are varied, including quick-frying, sautéing, frying and stirring in prepared sauce, deep-frying, stewing, braising, roasting, baking, spicing, marinating, smoking and coating, soaking, quick boiling, stirring and so on. The plate dressing style in Teochew cuisine is colorful and unique, as chefs would decorate dishes with flowers and birds carved from bamboo shoots, radishes or potatoes.

Teochew banquets are also distinctive. A big full banquet usually offers a feast of 12 courses, with two dimsums, one sweet and one salty. There must be two sweet dishes for a wedding banquet, indicating "being sweet from the beginning to the end". The arrangement creates a more delicious feast for guests and gives them a good mood.

Fish in bamboo tubes is one of the most traditional dishes in Teochew cuisine

Hakka Cuisine

Gourmet Food in Mountains

If Teochew cuisine is compared to girls living by the South China Sea who are pure and elegant, Hakka cuisines is like unsophisticated and steady girls in mountainous areas.

The ancestors of Hakka people left the Central Plains and made an arduous journey to settle down mostly in the mountainous areas of eastern Guangdong. Where there are mountains, there are Hakka people. As mountain dwellers, they live off the mountains. Hakka cuisine features the following six characteristics:

Hakka style brewed bean curd

Salty: Hakka dishes are usually a little salty; fat: hakka dishes are often soaked in oil and soup half and half; fragrant: the most-employed cooking methods are frying, deep-frying, sautéing and braising, in order to enhance the aroma of a dish; hot: dishes should be served when they are hot, and "being hot" is used as a criteria to judge whether a dish is delicious or not; well-done: dishes should be thoroughly cooked and shouldn't be served raw or half-cooked; preserved: pickled and preserved vegetables are popular since fresh ones would deteriorate during a long journey.

Hakka cuisine has the following four primary features: first, meat of domestic fowl and livestock, as well as of bushmeat, is the most-used ingredient. There is a saying: "Soup without chicken cannot be light, food without meat cannot be fragrant, dining without duck cannot be refreshing, and juice without pork leg cannot be mellow." Second, the main ingredient is the centerpiece in the curing process. The main food material is usually cut into chunks and cooked in a way to be soft, fragrant and mellow. Thick or strong-flavored seasonings are rarely or never added. Instead, raw scallion and cooked garlic are the commonly used condiments. Third, timing is given top priority in Hakka cuisine, and the best cooking techniques include stewing, toasting, simmering and braising. Hakka clay-pot casseroles are extremely famous. Fourth, the appearance of Hakka dishes is traditional-styled and unsophisticated with strong authentic local flavors.

Salt baked chicken is a typical Hakka dish

Eel with chives is a traditional Hakka dish

The traditional signature Hakka dishes include braised sliced pork with preserved vegetables, Hakka salt-baked chicken, Hakka stuffed tofu cubes (with minced meat), pork stomach wrapped chicken, stuffed bitter gourd, Poon Choy (Pot with assorted delicacies), Four Stars Longing for the Moon (Sliced carp steamed with scallions in a spicy sauce, surrounded by a quartet of smaller dishes), Hakka dumpling and Hakka steamed stuffed bun with taro. Different from Guangfu Cuisine and Teochew cuisine which underwent significant changes in the fusion of the Han and Yue cultures after the Qin Dynasty (221 B.C. –206 B.C.), Hakka cuisine has retained the traditions in the Central Plains, and some of its cooking techniques were inherited from the ancient practices and have evolved to thrive independently.

Food Traditions

Folk Customs

Guangfu Temple Fair

Boluodan Millennium Temple Fair

Qiqiao Festival

Dragon Boat Race

Open Air Banquet in Shunde

Guangfu Temple Fair

Guangfu Temple Fair, a traditional folk activity in Guangdong Province, has been newly upgraded by the city's Yuexiu District and become a one-week carnival held annually from the 15th day to the 21st day of the first lunar month on Chinese Calendar. Every year, the temple fair focuses on one specific theme. The theme of the 2015 event is "Get Together and Share the Happiness in Guangfu Temple Fair", which includes 10 activities like puppet performance, Chinese unique folk arts, martial arts performance and lantern show. It covers several elements of Chinese culture like blessings, folk customs, food and entertainment.

广府 忠信 庙会

舞龙队

Guangfu Temple Fair

Many unique activities of Guangfu traditions and culture can, again, find their way to the public arena through temple fairs. The most visited part of the temple fair is the gourmet area where many teahouses of unique style and time-honored brands would display their specialties to the visitors. The fair not only showcases famous local snacks but also traditional gourmet food that is further developed by Hong Kong and Macau. In 2015, the organizing committee of the temple fair, in cooperation with renowned food companies along the core culture zone in Beijing Road, developed an O2O business model for Guangfu cuisine that greatly promoted their growth.

Gourmet area of Guangfu Temple Fair

Boluodan Millennium Temple Fair

People gather at the Nanhai Temple to enjoy the grand folklore and cultural events

With a history of over a thousand years, Guangzhou's Boluodan Millennium Temple Fair is one of the most influential folk events with unique traditions of Han nationality in the Pearl River Delta Region, and is also China's only existing sacrificial ceremony dedicated to Mazu, Goddess of the Sea. It is held between the eleventh and the thirteenth day of the second lunar month on Chinese Calendar. The last day of the event, namely the thirteenth day of the second lunar month, is called Zhengdan, or Boluodan, meaning the birthday of Mazu.

During the fair, hundreds of thousands of visitors, including villagers in the Pearl River Delta Region as well as devout men and women, would come to the Nanhai God Temple, or South Sea

Visitors from all over the world gather around the Boluo Chicken at the Nanhai Temple

God Temple, for worshiping, sightseeing, shopping and enjoying delicious food. As a folk saying goes, " Visiting the Nanhai God Temple is more important than marrying a wife ", which demonstrates the significance of the temple fair.

Food festival during the temple fair is one of the most popular events. The food court, located in the front door of Nanhai God Temple, not only serves gourmet food and delicious snacks in Guangdong, Hong Kong and Macau, but also provides delicious food from all over China like Hangzhou, Xinjiang, Dalian, Fujian, Shaanxi and Taiwan. Moreover, the food festival also features unique cuisine across the globe, like those from Argentina and Brazil, which is a real bonus for foodies.

In recent years, local government has stepped up its efforts in applying for national intangible cultural heritage. In June, 2011, Boluodan traditional folk custom was included in the Third National Intangible Cultural Heritage List issued by the State Council.

Qiqiao Festival

Tribute of Qiqiao Festival

Guangzhou boasts the grandest celebration of Qiqiao Festival in China. It covers major procedures like worshiping the celestial beings, praying for wisdom from the Weaver Maid, reciting traditional prayers for dexterity in needlework, having fancy dinner known as the Weaver Maid's feast, and watching traditional operas known as the Weaver Maid's performance. The festival focuses on worshiping the celestial beings for cleverness in needlework and marital bliss, which calls for handicraft making including Qixi mascots and Magpie Bridge in miniature. Guangzhou's unique worshiping procedures in the Qiqiao Festival are not only toward the Altair and Vega stars, known respectively in Chinese folklore as the Cowherd and the Weaver Maid, but also the latter's six sisters, which greatly demonstrates the local custom of gods worshiping.

Qiqiao Festival covers major procedures like worshiping the celestials

People in Guangzhou have long attached much importance to celebrating this festival. As Liu Kezhuang, a poet in Southern Song Dynasty (1127–1279) wrote, Cantonese celebrate Qiqiao Festival all night long. From the late Qing Dynasty to the early Republic of China, the celebration was especially popular among the general public. There are a lot of folk songs dedicated to this theme and Guangzhou has gradually developed several street dedicated to selling needlework items.

Normally, married women are not allowed to participate in the Qiqiao Festival. However, newly-married women should take part in a ceremony in the first Qiqiao Festival after their marriage. During the ceremony, the newly-married should offer pears to gods, which means bidding farewell to maidenhood, and also offer sweet wine, red eggs and pickled ginger, which symbolizes productivity and fertility.

Dragon Boat Race

A Dragon Boat feast will be served to the contestants
and organizers of the event

Dragon Boat Race is a cultural sport event which enjoys a long
history in the Pearl River Delta Region. In late April every Chinese
lunar year, every town in the region would pick an auspicious
day to give sacrifice in the temple and then the eldest man in the
community would lead other young man to get the dragon boat
which was hidden in the dock last year out. Later on, the most
respected senior in the village will clean the boat and almost 80
strong villagers will begin practicing in it before the race.

Dragon Boat Race

On the fifth day of the fifth month of Chinese Lunar Calendar, teams from every town will compete in the race. The winner will be awarded with spirits and roasted pig for dinner. A Dragon Boat feast will be served to the contestants and organizers of the event. After dinner and a sacrificial ceremony, the dragon boat will be buried into the original dragon boat dock. The general practice for preparing Dragon Boat feast is to select several excellent cooks from the village who will deliver a delicious meal with all kinds of meat dishes like fish, pork, chicken and duck. The names of those dishes are also very auspicious, like lucky roasted pork.

Open Air Banquet in Shunde

The traditional open air banquet is the reflection of Cantonese food culture and also the extension of Lingnan's unique culture of ancestral worship.

This open air banquet cannot possibly work out single-handedly but calls for teamwork from volunteers of the community. It can be compared to an assembly line that needs manpower to engage in organization of the feast, preparation of the food and cleanup of dishes.

There are eight Cantonese classic dishes and one soup in every round of the banquet. Nowadays, this open air banquet has added one more procedure for diners after they finished their meals—they have to clean all the oil stains on their napkins for the next round of diners. It is quite spectacular to see hundreds of diners washing napkins at the same time and this group behavior is said to symbolize happiness and auspiciousness for the coming new year.

Open Air Banquet in Shunde

Local Specialties

Fruit and Tea

Lychee

Longan

Pineapple

Wampee

Chaoshan Kungfu Tea

Herbal Tea

Lei Cha (Ground Tea)

Lychee

Lychee, dubbed as the king of fruit in Asia, is very popular among Chinese people due to its sweet flavor and fragrant smell. As early as Tang Dynasty (618–907), the fruit has become tribute to the royal family. As it was the favorite fruit of Emperor Li Longji's favored concubine Yang Yuhuan (Yang Guifei), the emperor had the fruit delivered to her at great expense to the capital. Compared to her, Su Dongpo, the master poet in Northern Song Dynasty (960–1127), was much luckier because he could "enjoy 300 lychees a day" as he was demoted to the Lingnan region, something of a blessing in disguise. Since its flavor is lost in the process of transportation, lychee is better eaten fresh once picked up from the tree.

Lychees are extensively grown in China's Guangdong Province, and Maoming prefecture boasts the largest fruit production base in China and the largest lychee production base in the world with a cultivation area of 1,765,700 mu, or 117,713.33 hectares. Huilai County, the largest lychee production area in eastern Guangdong, has been named "hometown of lychees". Qianqiuzhen Village, Kuitan Town in Huilai County is home to lychee trees with a history of over a thousand years.

Longan

Longan is dubbed as one of the four famous fruit in Lingnan region, along with lychee, banana and pineapple. The longan is so named because it resembles an eyeball when its fruit is shelled (the black seed shows through the translucent flesh like an iris). The fruit is also called Guiyuan, as it is harvested on August and its shape is round.

Cultivation of longan can be traced back to the Han Dynasty (202 B.C.–A.D. 220) of about two thousand years ago, and was first documented in the *Book of Later Han*. Longan is one of the most well-known and well-used medicinal fruits in Chinese Medicine. It strengthens both the digestive system as well as the heart. This means that longan is especially good for blood deficiency symptoms that are related to mind or emotions. During the Han Dynasty, it has been widely used in Chinese Medicine. In the Ming Dynasty (1368–1644), the great medical doctor and herbalist Li Shizhen recognized the fruit as beneficial for people's health. It now enjoys wide application as one of the favored medicinal foods for insomnia, poor memory, stress and palpitation.

Pineapple

Pineapple is one of the four famous fruits in Lingnan region. It is very popular due to its sweet flavors and refreshing juicy texture.

Pineapple can be eaten fresh or in a processed form, notably canned ones which can preserve the original flavor of the fruit. It also finds application in culinary use like in the case of fried pork with pineapples and pineapple fried rice. Pineapples in those dishes facilitates digestion and makes them less greasy.

Xuwen County in Guangdong Province boasts a pineapple production base with its cultivation area reached 250,000 *mu* (16,666.67 hectares). The pineapples produced here, notably the ones grown in Yugonglou, are big, juicy, crispy and sweet. The county produces more than 340,000 tons of pineapples every year, ranking first in terms of total production in China. Its fresh and processed pineapples are popular at home and abroad. Canned pineapples now are exported to 60 countries and regions all over the world including Europe, America, the Middle East, Africa and the Oceania.

Wampee

Wampee, with a cultivation history of 1500 years, is a highly-esteemed fruit in southern China, where sour, sub-acid and sweet varieties are known. Some varieties have a sweet-sour flavor and juicy texture which can match lychee in terms of color, aroma and taste.

As a Cantonese proverb goes, "Lychees can feed your hunger while wampees can help digestion". Cantonese viewed the fruit as a God-sent treasure which can help produce saliva, slake thirst and facilitate digestion. Moreover, boiled wampee leaves can also be used to prevent colds and flu. Also, the root of wampee trees can be used to cure pain in one's body. Its skin and kernel, which can be diuretic and reduce swelling, is widely applied in Chinese Medicine. Other therapeutic qualities consist of coolant, stomachic, as well as antihelmintic.

Chaoshan Kungfu Tea

Kungfu Tea, with a literal meaning of "making tea with effort", is the most popular drink in Guangdong's Chaoshan region. According to ancient documents, the tea can be traced back to the Ming Dynasty and is well-established in the Qing Dynasty. During the Mid Qing Dynasty, it becomes a popular drink in the Chaoshan region and quickly spread to the neighboring areas like the Southeast Asia. Kungfu Tea is an integral part of Chaoshan's traditional culture. However, the tea processing technique has been replaced by instant tea in this fast-paced society.

Kungfu Tea

The making of Chaoshan Kungfu Tea includes several procedures like selecting high quality tea, choosing pure water, selecting the right kind of tea sets and brewing the tea in hot water. The brewing procedures is the most complicated one which includes preparing tea sets and tea leaves, brewing tea leaves, rinsing tea leaves, heating the teapot and tea cups and pouring the tea to the cups for later enjoyment. A very important part is to smell the aroma of the tea by inhaling the steam. After smelling, drink by taking small sips that allow to fully enjoy the taste, aroma and quality of the tea. Normally Chaoshan people would use oolong tea to make the drink.

Kungfu tea can be enjoyed in any circumstances and forms. It represents major part of China's tea culture with historical, cultural, aesthetic and entertainment value.

Herbal Tea

Herbal tea shop in Guangzhou

Since ancient times, the Cantonese have been famous for drinking herbal tea. Herbal tea is not kind of tea, but medicine soup boiled down from Chinese herbal medicine. Herbal tea is not necessarily cold and it works better to drink it hot. The most representative is Bansha Herbal Tea.

Herbal tea preparation techniques, handed down from generation to generation in a family tradition, have a history of hundreds of years. The earliest Guangdong herbal tea is Wong Lo Kat Herbal Tea, invented by Wong Chat Bong from Heshan City of Guangdong Province in 1828 during the Qing Dynasty. Later, Wong Lo Kat Herbal Tea went abroad and has turned popular

Herbal tea

among the Chinese all over the world for more than 170 years. It is indeed the pioneer drinks for people to clear heat, remove toxin and regain beauty.

There are 54 recipes derived from the following 18 herbal tea brands: Wong Lo Kat, Shangqingyin, Jianshengtang, Denglao, Baiyuanshan, Huangzhenlong, Xuqixiu, Chunhetang, Jinhulu, Xingqun, Runxintang, Shaxi, Lishi, Qingxintang, Xinglinchun, Baoqingtang, Fuqingtang and Huangfuxing. These recipes and the herbal tea culture have been widely recognized among the public. For hundreds of years, a forest of herbal tea shops in Guangdong, Hong Kong and Macao have constituted a unique landscape of the Lingnan culture.

Herbal tea was included in the first batch of national intangible cultural heritage announced by the State Council in 2006. Now, it has been sold all over China and in nearly twenty countries including the US, Canada, France, Britain, Italy, Germany, Australia and New Zealand.

Lei Cha (Ground Tea)

Lei cha or ground tea is quite unique in the great and profound Chinese tea art. As the special food for Hakka people, it is one of the traditional cuisines among the Hakka in Guangdong Province and Guangxi Zhuang Autonomous Region. It can be taken not only as part of their regular diet, but also a delicacy to entertain guests.

Every kind of food culture is poetic expression and enlightenment of the philosophy of life. The production of Lei cha and its flavors fully demonstrate Hakka people's inheritance of Chinese traditional culture. Lei cha is actually a mix of tea leaves, rice, sesame, soybeans, peanuts, salt and orange peel, sometimes with Chinese herbal medicine included. Such ingredients are ground with a mortar and pestle into powder. Easy to produce, the tea

Lei cha, a living fossil in Chinese tea culture

tastes pure with a strong fragrant smell. It is also affordable and brings a lot of benefits. Due to a varying mix of ingredients, Lei cha can help people quench their thirst, feel cool and refreshing, relieve summer heat, strengthen the spleen, warm the stomach, nourish themselves and prolong life.

This book is the result of a co-publication agreement between Nanfang Daily Press (CHINA) and Paths International Ltd. (UK)

Title: Cantonese Cuisine: A Bite of Freshness & Naturalness
Author: Elegant Guangdong Series Editorial Board
Hardback ISBN: 978-1-84464-724-8
Paperback ISBN: 978-1-84464-725-5
Ebook ISBN: 978-1-84464-726-2
Copyright © 2022 by Paths International Ltd., UK and by Nanfang Daily Press, China

Paths International Ltd
www.pathsinternational.com

Published in United Kingdom